Cryptocurrency Transaction Ledger

Cryptocurrency Transaction Ledger

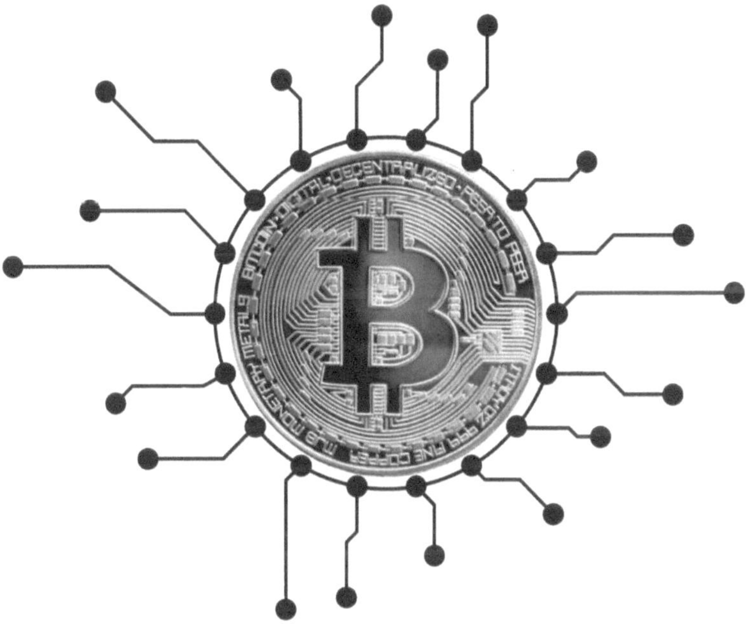

FUTURE FAMILY
PUBLISHING

Cryptocurrency Transaction Ledger
by Brenda Chunga

ISBN (Paperback): 978-0-9984447-6-5

Meet Brenda

Brenda Chunga is a world-renowned cryptocurrency enthusiast sought by some of the world's most successful cryptocurrency platforms. Her expertise in the space quickly propelled her status as a crypto-educator.

Once a single, unemployed mother of two, Brenda's hunger and passion for learning put her on a path that would change her life forever – taking her from unemployed to millionaire – all thanks to cryptocurrency.

Brenda teaches others to do what she did through her weekly webinars and online videos. Her specialized trainings allow followers to get a front seat to her in-depth knowledge and expertise in this volatile yet lucrative monetary vehicle called cryptocurrency.

The ***Cryptocurrency Transaction Ledger*** is a simple but effective tool that will assist you in building your crypto portfolio. Organization is one of the keys to success, and by using this ledger, you'll be able to track and organize all crypto transactions, exchanges, coins, and wallets.

Introduction

The key to being successful in the crypto space is organization, and with this transaction ledger in your hand, you are already on your way to becoming a savvy crypto enthusiast.

My philosophy when it comes to being successful in this business is utilizing practical tools that will help you build and organize business. It's imperative to establish and maintain an organized transaction ledger in order to avoid potential tax implications. No matter how large or small the transaction, you should track your receipts. This transaction ledger will assist you in doing just that.

I, too, keep a transaction ledger in order to stay on top of business. Remember, one of the keys to success is organization.

Brenda Chunga

Transaction Ledger

NAME Jane Smith

DATE January 30, 2022

RECEIVE X SENT

BORROW X LEND

CRYPTO

○ WALLET Crypto.com

○ CHAIN Etherium

○ AMOUNT 10,000

NAME

DATE

RECEIVE SENT

BORROW LEND

Something to Remember:

Burning: You burn cryptocurrencies by sending them to a wallet that can only receive cryptocurrencies. This typically has a deflationary impact causing the tokens in circulation to automatically increase in scarcity and value.

CRYPTO

○ WALLET

○ CHAIN

○ AMOUNT

NAME

DATE

RECEIVE SENT

BORROW LEND

CRYPTO

○ WALLET

○ CHAIN

○ AMOUNT

NOTES

Transaction Ledger

NAME

DATE

CRYPTO

○ WALLET

○ CHAIN

○ AMOUNT

RECEIVE SENT

BORROW LEND

NAME

DATE

CRYPTO

○ WALLET

○ CHAIN

○ AMOUNT

RECEIVE SENT

BORROW LEND

Something to Remember:

Chain Linking: All cryptocurrencies have their own blockchain network, which is actually a digital ledger for storing all transaction records. With chain linking, you can transfer or exchange two cryptocurrencies for each other.

NAME

DATE

RECEIVE SENT

BORROW LEND

CRYPTO

○ WALLET

○ CHAIN

○ AMOUNT

NOTES

Transaction Ledger

NAME

DATE

CRYPTO

○ WALLET

○ CHAIN

○ AMOUNT

RECEIVE SENT

BORROW LEND

NAME

DATE

RECEIVE SENT

BORROW LEND

Something to Remember:

Deterministic Wallet: It is the type of crypto wallet that can be created by generating multiple keys from a particular seed. In case you lose the deterministic wallet, the seed can help in recovering your wallet key.

CRYPTO

○ WALLET

○ CHAIN

○ AMOUNT

NAME

DATE

RECEIVE SENT

BORROW LEND

CRYPTO

○ WALLET

○ CHAIN

○ AMOUNT

NOTES

Transaction Ledger

NAME

DATE

CRYPTO

○ WALLET

○ CHAIN

○ AMOUNT

RECEIVE SENT

BORROW LEND

NAME

DATE

CRYPTO

○ WALLET

○ CHAIN

○ AMOUNT

RECEIVE SENT

BORROW LEND

Something to Remember:

ERC: It is an acronym for Ethereum Request for Comment. It's a method made for communication about the technical notes and requirements relevant to a group of users and developers. As of now, there are tens of thousands of different crypto tokens working on the precedents of the ERC-20 standard.

NAME

DATE

RECEIVE SENT

BORROW LEND

CRYPTO

○ WALLET

○ CHAIN

○ AMOUNT

NOTES

Transaction Ledger

NAME

DATE

RECEIVE SENT

BORROW LEND

CRYPTO

○ WALLET

○ CHAIN

○ AMOUNT

NAME

DATE

RECEIVE SENT

BORROW LEND

Something to Remember:

Ethereum: Ethereum features two important similarities with Bitcoin in that it is open source and relies on a blockchain technology foundation. However, it also differs from Bitcoin considerably by allowing developers to write smart contracts and develop decentralized applications on Ethereum.

CRYPTO

○ WALLET

○ CHAIN

○ AMOUNT

NAME

DATE

RECEIVE SENT

BORROW LEND

CRYPTO

○ WALLET

○ CHAIN

○ AMOUNT

NOTES

Transaction Ledger

NAME

DATE

CRYPTO

○ WALLET

○ CHAIN

○ AMOUNT

RECEIVE SENT

BORROW LEND

NAME

DATE

CRYPTO

○ WALLET

○ CHAIN

○ AMOUNT

RECEIVE SENT

BORROW LEND

Something to Remember:

Futures Contract: It is a pre-approved contract among two entities to complete a transaction in the event of the cryptocurrency value reaching a specific price. The futures contract is different from limit orders as the buyer and seller are already selected and bound to the contract.

NAME

DATE

RECEIVE SENT

BORROW LEND

CRYPTO

○ WALLET

○ CHAIN

○ AMOUNT

NOTES

Transaction Ledger

NAME

DATE

RECEIVE SENT

BORROW LEND

CRYPTO

○ WALLET

○ CHAIN

○ AMOUNT

NAME

DATE

RECEIVE SENT

BORROW LEND

Something to Remember:

Liquidity: It's the general term used in financial markets for defining the ease of converting an asset into cash. In the case of cryptocurrencies, liquidity refers to the ease of converting a crypto coin to other coins or fiat currencies.

CRYPTO

○ WALLET

○ CHAIN

○ AMOUNT

NAME

DATE

RECEIVE SENT

BORROW LEND

CRYPTO

○ WALLET

○ CHAIN

○ AMOUNT

NOTES

Transaction Ledger

NAME

DATE

CRYPTO

○ WALLET

○ CHAIN

○ AMOUNT

RECEIVE SENT

BORROW LEND

NAME

DATE

CRYPTO

○ WALLET

○ CHAIN

○ AMOUNT

RECEIVE SENT

BORROW LEND

Something to Remember:

Rug pulls: This is one of the most common types of attacks in the cryptocurrency space. Instances of rug pulls are evident when a specific cryptocurrency creator vanishes without any trace of the user's funds. Developers launch a new cryptocurrency in an ICO and then disappear without any trace after raising a hefty capital.

NAME

DATE

RECEIVE SENT

BORROW LEND

CRYPTO

○ WALLET

○ CHAIN

○ AMOUNT

NOTES

Transaction Ledger

NAME

DATE

RECEIVE SENT

BORROW LEND

CRYPTO

○ WALLET

○ CHAIN

○ AMOUNT

NAME

DATE

RECEIVE SENT

BORROW LEND

Something to Remember:

Decentralized Finance (DeFi): It's a combination of smart contracts operating independently on blockchains like the Ethereum network.

CRYPTO

○ WALLET

○ CHAIN

○ AMOUNT

NAME

DATE

RECEIVE SENT

BORROW LEND

CRYPTO

○ WALLET

○ CHAIN

○ AMOUNT

NOTES

Transaction Ledger

NAME

DATE

CRYPTO

○ WALLET

○ CHAIN

○ AMOUNT

RECEIVE SENT

BORROW LEND

NAME

DATE

CRYPTO

○ WALLET

○ CHAIN

○ AMOUNT

RECEIVE SENT

BORROW LEND

Something to Remember:

Audit: It refers to an internal or independent review of a specific concept, product, system, company, or process. The audit process deals with an insightful and detailed overview of various factors. The factors include the structure, vulnerabilities, strength, and weaknesses of the process or object under audit.

NAME

DATE

RECEIVE SENT

BORROW LEND

CRYPTO

○ WALLET

○ CHAIN

○ AMOUNT

NOTES

Transaction Ledger

NAME

DATE

RECEIVE SENT

BORROW LEND

CRYPTO

○ WALLET

○ CHAIN

○ AMOUNT

NAME

DATE

RECEIVE SENT

BORROW LEND

Something to Remember:

Stablecoin: It is a digital cryptocurrency that is equivalent in value to one USD. Stablecoin can make the DeFi sector an attractive investment.

CRYPTO

○ WALLET

○ CHAIN

○ AMOUNT

NAME

DATE

RECEIVE SENT

BORROW LEND

CRYPTO

○ WALLET

○ CHAIN

○ AMOUNT

NOTES

Transaction Ledger

NAME

DATE

CRYPTO

○ WALLET

○ CHAIN

○ AMOUNT

RECEIVE SENT

BORROW LEND

NAME

DATE

CRYPTO

○ WALLET

○ CHAIN

○ AMOUNT

RECEIVE SENT

BORROW LEND

Something to Remember:

Web 3.0: It's the third-generation of the internet. The central theme of Web 3.0 focuses on decentralization, thereby excluding any centralized sources of assets such as money, like modern banks.

NAME

DATE

RECEIVE SENT

BORROW LEND

CRYPTO

○ WALLET

○ CHAIN

○ AMOUNT

NOTES

Transaction Ledger

NAME

DATE

RECEIVE SENT

BORROW LEND

CRYPTO

○ WALLET

○ CHAIN

○ AMOUNT

NAME

DATE

RECEIVE SENT

BORROW LEND

Something to Remember:

Blockchain: A digital record of transactions that is impossible to cheat, change or hack.

CRYPTO

○ WALLET

○ CHAIN

○ AMOUNT

NAME

DATE

RECEIVE SENT

BORROW LEND

CRYPTO

○ WALLET

○ CHAIN

○ AMOUNT

NOTES

Transaction Ledger

NAME

DATE

CRYPTO

○ WALLET

○ CHAIN

○ AMOUNT

RECEIVE SENT

BORROW LEND

NAME

DATE

CRYPTO

○ WALLET

○ CHAIN

○ AMOUNT

RECEIVE SENT

BORROW LEND

Something to Remember:

Coinbase: A unique type of Bitcoin transaction with no inputs that is created by miners after finding new blocks. This type of transaction is, in most cases, the first transaction within new a block. Coinbase transactions reward miners for their work.

NAME

DATE

RECEIVE SENT

BORROW LEND

CRYPTO

○ WALLET

○ CHAIN

○ AMOUNT

NOTES

Transaction Ledger

NAME

DATE

RECEIVE SENT

BORROW LEND

CRYPTO

○ WALLET

○ CHAIN

○ AMOUNT

NAME

DATE

RECEIVE SENT

BORROW LEND

Something to Remember:

Cold Storage: A way to hold or store a digital asset offline—without connection to the internet. Typical cold storage includes USB drives, offline computers, or paper wallets. Cold storage is the safest method of storing your cryptocurrency especially for wallet balances that you plan to keep untouched for a significant period of time.

CRYPTO

○ WALLET

○ CHAIN

○ AMOUNT

NAME

DATE

RECEIVE SENT

BORROW LEND

CRYPTO

○ WALLET

○ CHAIN

○ AMOUNT

NOTES

Transaction Ledger

NAME

DATE

CRYPTO

○ WALLET

○ CHAIN

○ AMOUNT

RECEIVE SENT

BORROW LEND

NAME

DATE

CRYPTO

○ WALLET

○ CHAIN

○ AMOUNT

RECEIVE SENT

BORROW LEND

Something to Remember:

Confirmation(s): A bitcoin transaction is confirmed once it has been included in a block on the blockchain by a miner. Each subsequent block added to the blockchain is another confirmation for that transaction. 6+ confirmations is generally accepted for a transaction to be finalized.

NAME

DATE

RECEIVE SENT

BORROW LEND

CRYPTO

○ WALLET

○ CHAIN

○ AMOUNT

NOTES

Transaction Ledger

NAME

DATE

RECEIVE SENT

BORROW LEND

CRYPTO

○ WALLET

○ CHAIN

○ AMOUNT

NAME

DATE

RECEIVE SENT

BORROW LEND

Something to Remember:

Cosigner: A person or entity that has partial control over a multi-signature Bitcoin wallet. To complete a send of bitcoin, a multi-sig wallet requires authorization from a certain amount of all cosigners on the wallet.

CRYPTO

○ WALLET

○ CHAIN

○ AMOUNT

NAME

DATE

RECEIVE SENT

BORROW LEND

CRYPTO

○ WALLET

○ CHAIN

○ AMOUNT

NOTES

Transaction Ledger

NAME

DATE

RECEIVE SENT

BORROW LEND

CRYPTO

○ WALLET

○ CHAIN

○ AMOUNT

NAME

DATE

RECEIVE SENT

BORROW LEND

CRYPTO

○ WALLET

○ CHAIN

○ AMOUNT

Something to Remember:

Cryptocurrency: A digital currency that uses cryptography to provide security and verify transactions on its network. Unlike traditional fiat currencies, a cryptocurrency does not require a central bank or any other centralized authority to ensure security or to maintain control of money supply.

NAME

DATE

RECEIVE SENT

BORROW LEND

CRYPTO

○ WALLET

○ CHAIN

○ AMOUNT

NOTES

Transaction Ledger

NAME

DATE

RECEIVE SENT

BORROW LEND

CRYPTO

○ WALLET

○ CHAIN

○ AMOUNT

NAME

DATE

RECEIVE SENT

BORROW LEND

Something to Remember:

Cryptography: The practice and study of techniques for secure communication in the presence of third parties. Cryptography creates and secures wallets, signs all transactions, and verifies each and every transaction on the blockchain.

CRYPTO

○ WALLET

○ CHAIN

○ AMOUNT

NAME

DATE

RECEIVE SENT

BORROW LEND

CRYPTO

○ WALLET

○ CHAIN

○ AMOUNT

NOTES

Transaction Ledger

NAME

DATE

RECEIVE SENT

BORROW LEND

CRYPTO

○ WALLET

○ CHAIN

○ AMOUNT

NAME

DATE

RECEIVE SENT

BORROW LEND

CRYPTO

○ WALLET

○ CHAIN

○ AMOUNT

Something to Remember:

Decentralized: A form of organization which does not require any single party, group, or authority to control services. Bitcoin is a decentralized network because no company, government, or individual created or is in control of it. Bitcoin's governance relies on the community and its code is open-source.

NAME

DATE

RECEIVE SENT

BORROW LEND

CRYPTO

○ WALLET

○ CHAIN

○ AMOUNT

NOTES

Transaction Ledger

NAME

DATE

RECEIVE SENT

BORROW LEND

CRYPTO

○ WALLET

○ CHAIN

○ AMOUNT

NAME

DATE

RECEIVE SENT

BORROW LEND

Something to Remember:

Distributed: A distributed network does require users to connect to any central server or entity. In a distributed network, users connect directly to each other. Bitcoin is a distributed network that does not have any central processing entity.

CRYPTO

○ WALLET

○ CHAIN

○ AMOUNT

NAME

DATE

RECEIVE SENT

BORROW LEND

CRYPTO

○ WALLET

○ CHAIN

○ AMOUNT

NOTES

Transaction Ledger

NAME

DATE

RECEIVE SENT

BORROW LEND

CRYPTO

○ WALLET

○ CHAIN

○ AMOUNT

NAME

DATE

RECEIVE SENT

BORROW LEND

CRYPTO

○ WALLET

○ CHAIN

○ AMOUNT

Something to Remember:

Encryption/Encrypt: A crypto network uses cryptography to secure wallets so that only those in control of the private key associated with that wallet may access it to send Bitcoin from that address.

NAME

DATE

RECEIVE SENT

BORROW LEND

CRYPTO

○ WALLET

○ CHAIN

○ AMOUNT

NOTES

Transaction Ledger

NAME

DATE

RECEIVE SENT

BORROW LEND

CRYPTO

○ WALLET

○ CHAIN

○ AMOUNT

NAME

DATE

RECEIVE SENT

BORROW LEND

Something to Remember:

Exchange: A service, usually a website, that allows users to buy, sell, and trade cryptocurrencies.

CRYPTO

○ WALLET

○ CHAIN

○ AMOUNT

NAME

DATE

RECEIVE SENT

BORROW LEND

CRYPTO

○ WALLET

○ CHAIN

○ AMOUNT

NOTES

Transaction Ledger

NAME

DATE

CRYPTO

○ WALLET

○ CHAIN

○ AMOUNT

RECEIVE SENT

BORROW LEND

NAME

DATE

CRYPTO

○ WALLET

○ CHAIN

○ AMOUNT

RECEIVE SENT

BORROW LEND

Something to Remember:

Hash: A mathematical process miners use on blocks to secure the network and maintain network security. "Hash" also refers to the unique identifier of a Bitcoin transaction.

NAME

DATE

RECEIVE SENT

BORROW LEND

CRYPTO

○ WALLET

○ CHAIN

○ AMOUNT

NOTES

Transaction Ledger

NAME

DATE

RECEIVE SENT

BORROW LEND

CRYPTO

○ WALLET

○ CHAIN

○ AMOUNT

NAME

DATE

RECEIVE SENT

BORROW LEND

Something to Remember:

Hot Wallet: Any crypto wallet running on an internet connected device is considered "hot" (as opposed to an offline or "cold" wallet). Hot wallets should be secured by users since the funds on these wallets are subject to security compromise from hostile users on the network.

CRYPTO

○ WALLET

○ CHAIN

○ AMOUNT

NAME

DATE

RECEIVE SENT

BORROW LEND

CRYPTO

○ WALLET

○ CHAIN

○ AMOUNT

NOTES

Transaction Ledger

NAME

DATE

CRYPTO

○ WALLET

○ CHAIN

○ AMOUNT

RECEIVE SENT

BORROW LEND

NAME

DATE

CRYPTO

○ WALLET

○ CHAIN

○ AMOUNT

RECEIVE SENT

BORROW LEND

Something to Remember:

Ledger: A list of IDs, transactions, time-stamps, balances, and other data related to a financial account. The Bitcoin blockchain is a unique ledger in that it is distributed, decentralized, and public.

NAME

DATE

RECEIVE SENT

BORROW LEND

CRYPTO

○ WALLET

○ CHAIN

○ AMOUNT

NOTES

Transaction Ledger

NAME

DATE

RECEIVE SENT

BORROW LEND

CRYPTO

○ WALLET

○ CHAIN

○ AMOUNT

NAME

DATE

RECEIVE SENT

BORROW LEND

Something to Remember:

M of N: The requisite number of cosigners needed to provide signatures (M) out of the total amount of cosigners (N) within a multi-signature wallet. A common M of N value is "2 of 3". This means of the three cosigners, any two are needed to authorize a signature.

CRYPTO

○ WALLET

○ CHAIN

○ AMOUNT

NAME

DATE

RECEIVE SENT

BORROW LEND

CRYPTO

○ WALLET

○ CHAIN

○ AMOUNT

NOTES

Transaction Ledger

NAME

DATE

RECEIVE SENT

BORROW LEND

CRYPTO

○ WALLET

○ CHAIN

○ AMOUNT

NAME

DATE

RECEIVE SENT

BORROW LEND

CRYPTO

○ WALLET

○ CHAIN

○ AMOUNT

Something to Remember:

Miner: A specialized Bitcoin user comprised of a computer or group of computers that 1) collect pending transactions into blocks in order to process them and 2) verify blocks created by other miners. Miners are incentivized to perform this work because they collect all transaction fees and are rewarded with new bitcoins.

NAME

DATE

RECEIVE SENT

BORROW LEND

CRYPTO

○ WALLET

○ CHAIN

○ AMOUNT

NOTES

Transaction Ledger

NAME

DATE

RECEIVE SENT

BORROW LEND

CRYPTO

○ WALLET

○ CHAIN

○ AMOUNT

NAME

DATE

RECEIVE SENT

BORROW LEND

Something to Remember:

Multi-Signature: Also known as 'multisig'. These are bitcoin transactions that require authorizing signatures from multiple parties. Bitcoin.com wallets offer the multisig feature.

CRYPTO

○ WALLET

○ CHAIN

○ AMOUNT

NAME

DATE

RECEIVE SENT

BORROW LEND

CRYPTO

○ WALLET

○ CHAIN

○ AMOUNT

NOTES

Transaction Ledger

NAME

DATE

CRYPTO

○ WALLET

○ CHAIN

○ AMOUNT

RECEIVE SENT

BORROW LEND

NAME

DATE

CRYPTO

○ WALLET

○ CHAIN

○ AMOUNT

RECEIVE SENT

BORROW LEND

Something to Remember:

Open Source: Freely distributed software the code of which is available to the public to edit, use, and share. The Bitcoin code is open source.

NAME

DATE

RECEIVE SENT

BORROW LEND

CRYPTO

○ WALLET

○ CHAIN

○ AMOUNT

NOTES

Transaction Ledger

NAME

DATE

RECEIVE SENT

BORROW LEND

CRYPTO

○ WALLET

○ CHAIN

○ AMOUNT

NAME

DATE

RECEIVE SENT

BORROW LEND

Something to Remember:

Paper Wallet: An offline, cold storage, wallet where private key(s) are printed onto a piece of paper or manually attached to some other physical medium for offline storage. This is one of the most secure ways of holding a cryptocurrency.

CRYPTO

○ WALLET

○ CHAIN

○ AMOUNT

NAME

DATE

RECEIVE SENT

BORROW LEND

CRYPTO

○ WALLET

○ CHAIN

○ AMOUNT

NOTES

Transaction Ledger

NAME

DATE

RECEIVE SENT

BORROW LEND

CRYPTO

○ WALLET

○ CHAIN

○ AMOUNT

NAME

DATE

RECEIVE SENT

BORROW LEND

CRYPTO

○ WALLET

○ CHAIN

○ AMOUNT

Something to Remember:

Peer to Peer: A type of network where participants communicate directly with each other rather than through a centralized server. The Bitcoin network is a peer to peer network.

NAME

DATE

RECEIVE SENT

BORROW LEND

CRYPTO

○ WALLET

○ CHAIN

○ AMOUNT

NOTES

Transaction Ledger

NAME

DATE

RECEIVE SENT

BORROW LEND

CRYPTO

○ WALLET

○ CHAIN

○ AMOUNT

NAME

DATE

RECEIVE SENT

BORROW LEND

Something to Remember:

Alt Coin: An alt coin is anything that's not bitcoin.

CRYPTO

○ WALLET

○ CHAIN

○ AMOUNT

NAME

DATE

RECEIVE SENT

BORROW LEND

CRYPTO

○ WALLET

○ CHAIN

○ AMOUNT

NOTES

Transaction Ledger

NAME

DATE

CRYPTO

○ WALLET

○ CHAIN

○ AMOUNT

RECEIVE SENT

BORROW LEND

NAME

DATE

CRYPTO

○ WALLET

○ CHAIN

○ AMOUNT

RECEIVE SENT

BORROW LEND

Something to Remember:

Block: A group of data within a blockchain. Each block can only hold a certain amount of information.

NAME

DATE

RECEIVE SENT

BORROW LEND

CRYPTO

○ WALLET

○ CHAIN

○ AMOUNT

NOTES

Transaction Ledger

NAME

DATE

CRYPTO

○ WALLET

○ CHAIN

○ AMOUNT

RECEIVE SENT

BORROW LEND

NAME

DATE

RECEIVE SENT

BORROW LEND

Something to Remember:

Decentralized Applications: DApps are applications designed by developers and deployed on the blockchain to carry out actions without intermediaries

CRYPTO

○ WALLET

○ CHAIN

○ AMOUNT

NAME

DATE

RECEIVE SENT

BORROW LEND

CRYPTO

○ WALLET

○ CHAIN

○ AMOUNT

NOTES

Transaction Ledger

NAME

DATE

RECEIVE SENT

BORROW LEND

CRYPTO

○ WALLET

○ CHAIN

○ AMOUNT

NAME

DATE

RECEIVE SENT

BORROW LEND

CRYPTO

○ WALLET

○ CHAIN

○ AMOUNT

Something to Remember:

Fork: When a block chain's user makes changes to its rules. These changes in protocol often result in two new paths on the blockchain. One that follows the old rules and one following the new.

NAME

DATE

RECEIVE SENT

BORROW LEND

CRYPTO

○ WALLET

○ CHAIN

○ AMOUNT

NOTES

Transaction Ledger

NAME

DATE

RECEIVE SENT

BORROW LEND

CRYPTO

○ WALLET

○ CHAIN

○ AMOUNT

NAME

DATE

RECEIVE SENT

BORROW LEND

Something to Remember:

Gas: A fee that developers have to pay the Ethereum network in order to use the system

CRYPTO

○ WALLET

○ CHAIN

○ AMOUNT

NAME

DATE

RECEIVE SENT

BORROW LEND

CRYPTO

○ WALLET

○ CHAIN

○ AMOUNT

NOTES

Transaction Ledger

NAME

DATE

CRYPTO

○ WALLET

○ CHAIN

○ AMOUNT

RECEIVE SENT

BORROW LEND

NAME

DATE

CRYPTO

○ WALLET

○ CHAIN

○ AMOUNT

RECEIVE SENT

BORROW LEND

Something to Remember:

Genesis Block: The first block of cryptocurrency ever mined.

NAME

DATE

RECEIVE SENT

BORROW LEND

CRYPTO

○ WALLET

○ CHAIN

○ AMOUNT

NOTES

Transaction Ledger

NAME

DATE

RECEIVE SENT

BORROW LEND

CRYPTO

○ WALLET

○ CHAIN

○ AMOUNT

NAME

DATE

RECEIVE SENT

BORROW LEND

Something to Remember:

HODL: Stands for "Hold On for Dear Life". It was a typo on a 2013 forum by a bitcoin user. It refers to a passive investment strategy where you hold on to cryptocurrency instead of trading it.

CRYPTO

○ WALLET

○ CHAIN

○ AMOUNT

NAME

DATE

RECEIVE SENT

BORROW LEND

CRYPTO

○ WALLET

○ CHAIN

○ AMOUNT

NOTES

Transaction Ledger

NAME

DATE

RECEIVE SENT

BORROW LEND

CRYPTO

○ WALLET

○ CHAIN

○ AMOUNT

NAME

DATE

RECEIVE SENT

BORROW LEND

CRYPTO

○ WALLET

○ CHAIN

○ AMOUNT

Something to Remember:

Halving: A feature written into bitcoins code in which after a certain number of blocks are mined (typically after 4 years) the number of new Bitcoins entering circulation gets halved.

NAME

DATE

RECEIVE SENT

BORROW LEND

CRYPTO

○ WALLET

○ CHAIN

○ AMOUNT

NOTES

Transaction Ledger

NAME

DATE

RECEIVE SENT

BORROW LEND

CRYPTO

○ WALLET

○ CHAIN

○ AMOUNT

NAME

DATE

RECEIVE SENT

BORROW LEND

Something to Remember:

Initial Coin Offering (ICO): A way that funds are raised for a new cryptocurrency project.

CRYPTO

○ WALLET

○ CHAIN

○ AMOUNT

NAME

DATE

RECEIVE SENT

BORROW LEND

CRYPTO

○ WALLET

○ CHAIN

○ AMOUNT

NOTES

Transaction Ledger

NAME

DATE

CRYPTO

○ WALLET

○ CHAIN

○ AMOUNT

RECEIVE SENT

BORROW LEND

NAME

DATE

CRYPTO

○ WALLET

○ CHAIN

○ AMOUNT

RECEIVE SENT

BORROW LEND

Something to Remember:

Market Capitalization: Often referred to as "Market Cap" refers to the total value of all the coins that have been mined. You can find Market Cap by multiplying the current number of coins by the current value of the coin.

NAME

DATE

RECEIVE SENT

BORROW LEND

CRYPTO

○ WALLET

○ CHAIN

○ AMOUNT

NOTES

Transaction Ledger

NAME

DATE

RECEIVE SENT

BORROW LEND

CRYPTO

○ WALLET

○ CHAIN

○ AMOUNT

NAME

DATE

RECEIVE SENT

BORROW LEND

Something to Remember:

Node: A computer that connects to the blockchain network.

CRYPTO

○ WALLET

○ CHAIN

○ AMOUNT

NAME

DATE

RECEIVE SENT

BORROW LEND

CRYPTO

○ WALLET

○ CHAIN

○ AMOUNT

NOTES

Transaction Ledger

NAME

DATE

RECEIVE SENT

BORROW LEND

CRYPTO

○ WALLET

○ CHAIN

○ AMOUNT

NAME

DATE

RECEIVE SENT

BORROW LEND

CRYPTO

○ WALLET

○ CHAIN

○ AMOUNT

Something to Remember:

Non-Fungible Token (NFT): Units of value used to represent the ownership of unique digital items like art or collectibles. They are most often held on the Ethereum blockchain.

NAME

DATE

RECEIVE SENT

BORROW LEND

CRYPTO

○ WALLET

○ CHAIN

○ AMOUNT

NOTES

Transaction Ledger

NAME

DATE

RECEIVE SENT

BORROW LEND

CRYPTO

○ WALLET

○ CHAIN

○ AMOUNT

NAME

DATE

RECEIVE SENT

BORROW LEND

Something to Remember:

Public Key: Your wallets address, which is similar to your bank account number. You share this key with people or institutions so they can send or take money from your account when you authorize it.

CRYPTO

○ WALLET

○ CHAIN

○ AMOUNT

NAME

DATE

RECEIVE SENT

BORROW LEND

CRYPTO

○ WALLET

○ CHAIN

○ AMOUNT

NOTES

Transaction Ledger

NAME

DATE

CRYPTO

○ WALLET

○ CHAIN

○ AMOUNT

RECEIVE SENT

BORROW LEND

NAME

DATE

CRYPTO

○ WALLET

○ CHAIN

○ AMOUNT

RECEIVE SENT

BORROW LEND

Something to Remember:

Private Key: 1the encrypted code that allows direct access to your cryptocurrency. Like a bank account password, you should never share your private key

NAME

DATE

RECEIVE SENT

BORROW LEND

CRYPTO

○ WALLET

○ CHAIN

○ AMOUNT

NOTES

Transaction Ledger

NAME

DATE

RECEIVE SENT

BORROW LEND

CRYPTO

○ WALLET

○ CHAIN

○ AMOUNT

NAME

DATE

RECEIVE SENT

BORROW LEND

Something to Remember:

Smart Contract: An algorithmic program that enacts the terms of a contract automatically based on its code

CRYPTO

○ WALLET

○ CHAIN

○ AMOUNT

NAME

DATE

RECEIVE SENT

BORROW LEND

CRYPTO

○ WALLET

○ CHAIN

○ AMOUNT

NOTES

Transaction Ledger

NAME

DATE

CRYPTO

○ WALLET

○ CHAIN

○ AMOUNT

RECEIVE SENT

BORROW LEND

NAME

DATE

CRYPTO

○ WALLET

○ CHAIN

○ AMOUNT

RECEIVE SENT

BORROW LEND

Something to Remember:

Satoshi Natomoto: The pseudonymous creator of Bitcoin. No one knows his true identity, or if its more than one person

NAME

DATE

RECEIVE SENT

BORROW LEND

CRYPTO

○ WALLET

○ CHAIN

○ AMOUNT

NOTES

Transaction Ledger

NAME

DATE

RECEIVE SENT

BORROW LEND

CRYPTO

○ WALLET

○ CHAIN

○ AMOUNT

NAME

DATE

RECEIVE SENT

BORROW LEND

Something to Remember:

Bitcoin Cash: A peer-to-peer electronic cash system that formed a fork of the original Bitcoin. Where bitcoin is seen as too volatile to be useful for currency, Bitcoin Cash is designed to be better optimized for transactions

CRYPTO

○ WALLET

○ CHAIN

○ AMOUNT

NAME

DATE

RECEIVE SENT

BORROW LEND

CRYPTO

○ WALLET

○ CHAIN

○ AMOUNT

NOTES

Crypto Cards

1. **Burning:** Cryptocurrencies are burned by sending them to a wallet that can only receive cryptocurrencies. This typically causes the tokens in circulation to automatically increase in scarcity and value.

2. **Chain linking:** All cryptocurrencies have their own blockchain network, which is actually a digital ledger for storing all transaction records. With chain linking, you can transfer or exchange two cryptocurrencies for each other.

3. **Genesis Drop:** A genesis drop is the first NFT or collection of NFTs released by a creator.

4. **White List:** In crypto, a whitelist is a list of approved participants for a particular ICO or NFT mint. Participants are linked to their wallet address, so you if you want to be whitelisted for an upcoming drop, you must submit or share your wallet address for the blockchain the issuer or creator is using.

5. **Ethereum:** Ethereum has two similarities with Bitcoin in that it is open source and relies on a blockchain technology foundation. However, it also differs from Bitcoin considerably by allowing developers to write smart contracts and develop decentralized applications on Ethereum.

6. **Futures Contract:** A pre-approved contract among two entities to complete a transaction in the event of the cryptocurrency value reaching a specific price. The futures contract is different from limit orders as the buyer and seller are already selected and bound to the contract.

7. **Liquidity:** It's the general term used in financial markets for defining the ease of converting an asset into cash. In the case of cryptocurrencies, liquidity refers to the ease of converting a crypto coin to other coins or fiat currencies.

8. **Rug Pulls:** This is one of the most common types of attacks in the cryptocurrency space. Instances of rug pulls are evident when a specific cryptocurrency creator vanishes without any trace of the user's funds. Developers launch a new cryptocurrency in an ICO and then disappear without any trace after raising a hefty capital.

9. **Know Your Customer (KYC):** Although not required, many crypto exchanges carry out certain identity checks on their customers under KYC rules.

10. **Audit:** The audit process deals with an insightful and detailed overview of various factors. The factors include the structure, vulnerabilities, strength, and weaknesses of the process or object under audit.

11. **Stable Coin:** It is a digital cryptocurrency that is equivalent in value to one USD. Stable Coins can make the DeFi sector an attractive investment.

12. **Web 3.0:** It's the third generation of the internet. The central theme of web 3.0 focuses on decentralization, thereby excluding any centralized sources of assets such as money, like modern banks.

13. **Blockchain:** A digital record of transactions that is impossible to cheat, change or hack.

14. **Fiat Currency:** Traditional currencies are backed by the full faith and credit of a nation-state. The U.S. dollar, the Euro or the British pound are fiat currencies.

15. **Cold Storage:** A way to hold or store a digital asset offline—without connection to the internet. Typical cold storage includes USB drives, offline computers, or paper wallets. Cold storage is the safest method of storing your cryptocurrency.

16. **Confirmation(s):** A bitcoin transaction is confirmed once it has been included in a block on the blockchain by a miner. Each subsequent block added to the blockchain is another confirmation for that transaction. 6+ confirmations is generally accepted for a transaction to be finalized.

17. **Cosigner:** A person or entity that has partial control over a multi-signature Bitcoin wallet. To complete a send of bitcoin, a multi-sig wallet requires authorization from a certain amount of all cosigners on the wallet.

18. **Cryptocurrency:** A digital currency that uses cryptography to provide security and verify transactions on its network. Unlike traditional fiat currencies, a cryptocurrency does not require a central bank or any other centralized authority to ensure the security or to maintain control of the money supply.

19. **Cryptography:** The practice and study of techniques for secure communication in the presence of third parties. Cryptography creates and secures wallets, signs all transactions, and verifies each and every transaction on the blockchain.

20. **Decentralized:** A form of organization that does not require any single party, group, or authority to control services. Bitcoin is a decentralized network because no company, government, or individual created or is in control of it. Bitcoin's governance relies on the community, and its code is open-source.

21. **Distributed:** A distributed network doesn't require users to connect to any central server or entity. In a distributed network, users connect directly to each other. Bitcoin is a distributed network that does not have any central processing entity.

22. **Encryption/Encrypt:** A crypto network uses cryptography to secure wallets so that only those in control of the private key associated with that wallet may access it to send Bitcoin from that address.

23. **Exchange:** A service, usually a website, that allows users to buy, sell, and trade cryptocurrencies.

24. **Hash:** A mathematical process miners use on blocks to secure the network and maintain network security. "Hash" also refers to the unique identifier of a Bitcoin transaction.

25. **Hot Wallet:** Any crypto wallet running on an internet-connected device is considered "hot." Hot wallets should be secured by users since the funds on these wallets are subject to security compromise from hostile users on the network.

26. **Ledger:** A list of IDs, transactions, time stamps, balances, and other data related to a financial account. The Bitcoin blockchain is a unique ledger in that it is distributed, decentralized, and public.

27. **Whale:** A whale is the term used for the most valuable Bitcoin addresses. There are about 2000 Bitcoin whale addresses, and only three own more than 100,000 BTC.

28. **Miner:** A specialized Bitcoin user comprised of a computer or group of computers that 1) collect pending transactions into blocks in order to process them and 2) verify blocks created by other miners. Miners are incentivized to perform this work because they collect all transaction fees and are rewarded with new bitcoins.

29. **Multi-Signature:** Also known as 'multisig'. These are bitcoin transactions that require authorizing signatures from multiple parties. Bitcoin.com wallets offer the multisig feature.

30. **Node:** A special participant on the Bitcoin network. Nodes hold a copy of the blockchain ledger and relay new transactions to other nodes. A computer that connects to the blockchain network.

31. **Open Source:** Freely distributed software, the code of which is available to the public to edit, use, and share. The Bitcoin code is open source.

32. **Paper Wallet:** An offline, cold storage wallet where private key(s) are printed onto a piece of paper or manually attached to some other physical medium for offline storage. This is one of the most secure ways of holding a cryptocurrency.

33. **Peer-to-Peer:** A type of network where participants communicate directly with each other rather than through a centralized server. The Bitcoin network is a peer-to-peer network.

34. **Alt Coin:** An alt coin is anything that's not bitcoin.

35. **Block:** A group of data within a blockchain. Each block can only hold a certain amount of information.

36. **Decentralized Applications:** DApps are applications designed by developers and deployed on the blockchain to carry out actions without intermediaries.

37. **Fork:** When a blockchain user makes changes to its rules. These changes in a protocol often result in two new paths on the blockchain. One that follows the old rules and one following the new.

38. **Gas:** a fee that developers have to pay the Ethereum network in order to use the system.

39. **Genesis Block:** The first block of cryptocurrency ever mined.

40. **HODL:** Stands for "Hold On for Dear Life". It was a typo on a 2013 forum by a bitcoin user. It refers to a passive investment strategy where you hold on to cryptocurrency instead of trading it.

41. **Halving:** A feature written into bitcoins code in which after a certain number of blocks are mined (typically after 4 years), the number of new Bitcoins entering circulation gets halved.

42. **Initial Coin Offering (ICO):** A way that funds are raised for a new cryptocurrency project.

43. **Market Capitalization:** Often referred to as "Market Cap," refers to the total value of all the coins that have been mined. You can find Market Cap by multiplying the current number of coins by the current value of the coin.

44. **Non-Fungible Token (NFT):** Units of value used to represent the ownership of unique digital items like art or collectibles. They are most often held on the Ethereum blockchain.

45. **Public Key:** Your wallets address, which is similar to your bank account number. You share this key with people or institutions so they can send or take money from your account when you authorize it.

46. **Private Key:** An encrypted code that allows direct access to your cryptocurrency. Like a bank account password, you should never share your private key.

47. **Smart Contract:** An algorithmic program that enacts the terms of a contract automatically based on its code.

46. **Private Key:** An encrypted code that allows direct access to your cryptocurrency. Like a bank account password, you should never share your private key.

47. **Smart Contract:** An algorithmic program that enacts the terms of a contract automatically based on its code.

48. **Satoshi Nakamoto:** The pseudonymous creator of Bitcoin. No one knows his true identity or if it's more than one person.

49. **Bitcoin Cash:** A peer-to-peer electronic cash system that formed a fork of the original Bitcoin. Where bitcoin is seen as too volatile to be useful for currency, Bitcoin Cash is designed to be better optimized for transactions.

50. **Recovery Seed:** A recovery seed is a series of twelve, sometimes sixteen words that can be used to access your wallet if something goes wrong and you lose it. Your recovery seed is the equivalent of asking twelve security questions for a forgotten password.

51. **Satoshi:** The smallest unit in Bitcoin (BTC). For example, 1 satoshi is equivalent to 0.00000001 BTC, a fraction of a penny.

52. **Tether (USDC):** A stablecoin that is pegged 1-to-1 with the U.S. dollar.

53. **Whitepaper:** A technical document released alongside new crypto projects that explains how the system works.

54. **Yield:** A return on investment, expressed as a percentage.

Made in United States
Troutdale, OR
11/03/2026

56847411R00037